C000246680

RAILFREIGHT

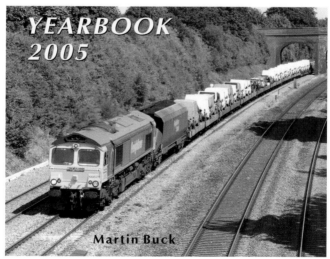

YEARBOOK 2005

Martin Buck

FREIGHTMASTER

PUBLISHING

CONTENTS

First published : April 2006

ISBN : 0-9537540-6-5

Published by : Freightmaster Publishing
158 Overbrook
SWINDON
SN3 6AY

01793 - 644957

Printed By : Stephens & George
MERTHYR TYDFIL

Cover design : Martin Buck / Steve Griffiths

INTRODUCTION

Background

RAILFREIGHT YEARBOOK - 2005, follows on from last years successful launch of FREIGHTMASTER REVIEW 1995 - 2004, which not only celebrated the first ten years of FREIGHTMASTER, but also documented the main freight developments that took place during that period.

This new book takes a *pictorial* look at the freight highlights of 2005 with high quality photographs to record the events. The book differs this time by covering more topics, such as diversions, Network Measurement Trains, Water Cannons, etc.

It is hoped that that this style of publication will become an annual event and, if this one proves successful, the 2006 title maybe expanded yet further to cover more loco-hauled events. So, watch this space!

Acknowledgement

I would like to thank all the people who have kindly contributed material for this book. In fact, I have been inundated with material, which has taken a very long (but rewarding) time to make a final selection. I know that some people will be disappointed in not being represented in the book, but the large number of contributors made this somewhat inevitable. The majority of contributors are Freightmaster Subscribers, so the selection reflects the areas of the country these people live/visit and the railfreight highlights they photographed for posterity.

About this book

For ease of reference, RAILFREIGHT YEARBOOK - 2005 is divided into eight chapters and a brief overview of each is given below; summarised in the same order as they appear in the following pages.

Freight Flows

This is the largest section with forty five pages devoted to recording the important freight flows which have come on stream during 2005. By way of example, Freightliner *Heavy Haul* continue to expand their aggregate business, especially out of Peak Forest, as well as the welcome return of Ellesmere Port to the railfreight map with a new flow of coal to Fiddlers Ferry Power Station.

EWS resume pipe traffic from Stanton Gate to Tees Dock and from Hartlepool to Leith and Georgemas Junction, along with supplies of steel to a new terminal at Bristol. Construction projects see stone to Gerrards Cross(!) along with the movement of flyash and brine relating to the Northwich stabilisation project.

GBRf continue to progress with daily gypsum trains over the Settle & Carlisle and take over the North Walsham condensate tanks. However, a major highlight is a move into Scotland, running a 'Mud Oil' train between Harwich and Aberdeen.

As for DRS, they introduce a new chemicals intermodal train service between Ditton and Purfleet and hire out locomotives for the seasonal Sandite workings.

About this book *(cont.)*

Diversions

Due to a variety of reasons, mostly as a result of engineering work, many freight services are diverted off their regular route. A selection are illustrated, including the annual weekend Spring diversions over the Settle & Carlisle and diversions via Chepstow as a result of the Patchway Tunnel blockade.

Specials

During the year there are many 'One-off' freight services including those which run under STP (Special Train Plan) arrangements. Highlights include:

- Freightliner running infrastructure trains to the Far North of Scotland
- Mail trains to Aberdeen during the World G8 conference at Gleneagles
- DRS move Hi-Cube wagons from Swindon to Carlisle
- Mail Trial and 325 units on the GWML

Plus, a small selection of pictures to illustrate the use of freight locomotives on rail enthusiast charter trains.

Locomotives

This section highlights the dwindling use of class 37s, including the sole 'booked' 37 turn - the Edinburgh 'Binliner'. DRS deem their Class 33 fleet to be substandard and EWS apply 'beastie' stickers to their non-EWS liveried locomotives. Freightliner withdraw No. 86220 after catching fire, place three Class 57s in store and repaint No. 90016 in their smart Green & Yellow livery.

The EWS celebrity Class 67 No. 67029 in slick silver-grey livery is depicted as this generates interest wherever it goes, along with the hire of Class 87s by GBRf for use on mail trains

Infrastructure

Here, we take a quick peep at two construction projects:

The LGV - SNCF high speed line to Strasbourg, as many UK rail enthusiasts visit France to observe ex-EWS Class 56 and Class 58 locomotives at work on infrastructure trains.

Stage 2 of the CTRL line in the London suburbs.

Measurement Trains / Stock Moves / Railhead Treatment Trains

These last three sections take a close look at areas of railfreight activity that generate a lot of interest, especially as they invariably feature motive power working away from their normal duties / routes.

This includes the introduction of new wagons, the movement of EMUs for scrap, Network Rail/Serco and Ultrasonic test trains, plus Water Cannons and Weedkilling trains throughout the network. A varied selection is included 'off the beaten track' featuring motive power from the four main railfreight operators.

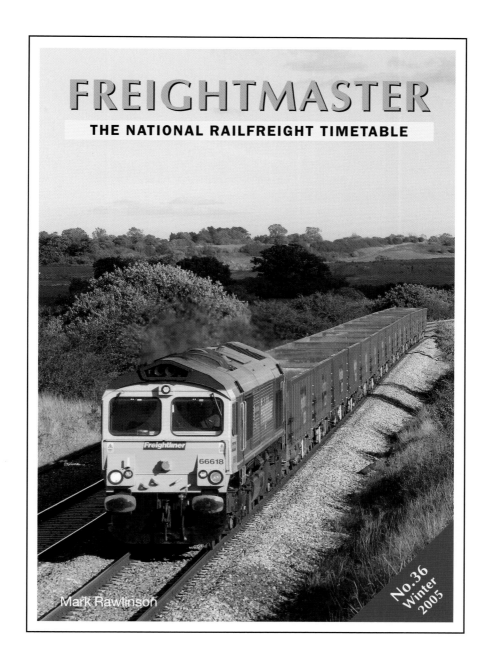

COAL

EWS

After many months absence and a change in ownership, Uskmouth Power Station (previously Fifoots) starts to receive supplies of MGR coal: the loaded services are listed below, but the returning 'empties' are excluded because they can be staged at East Usk pending a path into Newport Docks:

6F72, Newport Docks - Uskmouth

6F56, Newport Docks - Uskmouth

CONSTRUCTION MATERIALS

EWS

Stone :

a) The year begins with a contract to move stone for the construction of a tunnel to accommodate a new Tesco store at Gerrards Cross. A daily service runs from Acton, which is disrupted when the tunnel collapses in June, causing major disruption to Chiltern Line services:

7M36, Acton Yard - Gerrards Cross

7V37, Gerrards Cross - Acton Yard

b) EWS announce a 10 year contract with MendipRail to haul stone from Merehead and Whatley quarries to London terminals, which is the biggest contract EWS has secured for more than a year.

c) In conjunction with the expansion of Humber Import Terminal at Immingham, EWS will supply two trainloads of stone a week (TThO) in MBA box wagons from Doves Holes quarry in the Peak District:

6Z51, Peak Forest - Immingham

6Z15, Immingham - Peak Forest

d) Another short term flow commences from Bardon Hill quarry in Leicestershire to supply stone for the upgrading of the A1 into a full motorway near Ferrybridge, which includes a major new interchange with the M62. The stone is stockpiled at Gascoigne Wood, conveyed in a trainset comprising 32 MBAs.

6E50, Bardon Hill - Gascoigne Wood

6M51, Gascoigne Wood - Bardon Hill

Interestingly, FHH have agreed not to run their 6M17, Barrow Hill - Stud farm service whilst this new service runs, thereby allowing a path on the single line between Bagworth Junction and Knighton Junction. The flow is scheduled to finish by the end of the 2005 timetable.

Cement :

To demonstrate their commitment to cement, British Lime Industries (BLI) introduce new JGA tanks, which are initially used on the Tunstead - Walsall service. Furthermore, after a brief trial, regular deliveries of cement start running from Tunstead to a terminal at Willesden with both trains running via the WCML:

6A50, Tunstead - Willesden

6H50, Willesden - Tunstead

CONSTRUCTION MATERIALS *(continued)*

Flyash :

The first train of a new contract to supply flyash from Drax power station to infill the Salt mines under Northwich commences, running as:

6M27, Healey Mills - Northwich	6Z56, Northwich - Healey Mills

Both trains are routed via Stockport and are formed of MBA wagons. The outward train is initially being loaded at Selby Potter Group sidings until proper loading facilities can be installed at Drax. The wagons are 'tripped' between Selby and Healey Mills.

FHH

Lime :

Freightliner *Heavy Haul* continue to expand into the aggregates market by taking over the supply of lime to the desulphurisation plant at West Burton power station. Trains are formed of PGA 4-wheel hoppers and run as follows:

6Z56, Tunstead - West Burton	6Z55, West Burton - Barrow Hill

Stone :

A new trial flow commences, moving grit stone (a particularly hard stone used in making tarmac for road construction) from Jersey Marine to Burngullow which, if successful, will be a most welcome addition to freight services in Cornwall. Operationally, this working is interesting because the service has to split into two parts in Hackney Yard, Newton Abbot, in order to negotiate the ascent of Rattery! The trainplan is:

	6Z38, Kingsland Road - Jersey Marine
6Z39, Jersey Marine - Burngullow	6Z41, Hackney Yard - Burngullow
6Z43, Burngullow - Kingsland Road	

As an aside, it is also worth commenting in general on the growth in the number of stone trains now emanating out of South Wales . Including the Burngullow service, there can be upto 12 trains a week, compared to none ten years ago. One weekly example is as follows:-

MWFO	Moreton-on-Lugg - Hayes	TO	Machen - Westbury (2 services)
MO	Jersey Marine - Angerstein	TWTHO	Tower - Westbury
WO	Jersey Marine - Thorney Mill		

INTERMODAL

EWS

a) Last year, EWS suspended some of their intermodal services due to the threat of industrial action, which have now restarted, specifically the contract services for Argos and IKEA:

4Z79, Southampton W. D. - Burton on Trent	4Z22, Burton - Southampton W. D.
4M10, Southampton W. D. - Wembley	

4Z74, Wembley - Ely	4Z75, Ely - Wembley
4O05, Wembley - Southampton W. D.	

4H46, Felixstowe South - Ely	
4A27, Ely - Harwich	6R82, Harwich - Felixstowe South

b) Unfortunately, following the sale of Safeway's Scottish stores to Tesco / Somerfield, the 'Safeway' intermodal services no longer run, which means the following trans have been cancelled:

4H44, Mossend   - Georgemas Junction
6D65, Inverness   - Mossend
4D66, Georgemas Jct.   - Mossend
4H46, Georgemas Jct.   - Inverness
4D68, Inverness   - Mossend

On the plus side, a new service starts between Inverness and Mossend (4D05) and there is the possibility of Tesco running an intermodal service to Inverness in the near future!

FREIGHTLINER

FHH

a) Two new giant container cranes are commissioned at Widnes in order to handle the new 9ft. 6in. containers operated by Freightliner. The Liebherr cranes are part of an £ 8.5 million investment by the O,Connor Group, who operate the terminal. They will help increase capacity by more than 100,000 tonnes per annum and are capable of transferring over 1,000 containers each day between rail and road. As a result, two new trains are introduced in connection with the improved handling facilities at Ditton:

4M94, Felixstowe - Ditton   4L95, Ditton - Felixstowe

b) As a consequence of EWS taking over the Fort William Aluminium traffic, there is no longer a need to provide a Coatbridge connection into the daily Crewe to Cardiff freightliner service. So, the 4M27 service from Coatbridge to Crewe will be withdrawn and replaced by a new 4M74, Coatbridge - Crewe service. Any traffic for Seaforth going forward from Crewe the following morning on 4F82, Crewe - Seaforth.

METALS

EWS

a) EWS win the Aluminium traffic from Freightliner (who actually used road traffic to transport between Fort William and Coatbridge) and use the 'Enterprise' network to convey the ingots. This leads to an extra working on Saturdays on the West Highland Line:

6D16, Fort William - Mossend   6Y15, Mossend - Fort William

b) Some good news on the metals front .... Celsa steelworks at Cardiff has not dispatched much by rail, the most notable flow being the weekly trainload of steel bars to Colnbrook in connection with construction of Terminal 5 at Heathrow Airport. However, a new flow has commenced from Cardiff to Rotherham Steel Terminal:

6Z58, Cardiff Tidal - Rotherham   6Z67, Rotherham - Cardiff Tidal

c) Corus has won a major new contract to supply a 240km. gas pipeline to link the UK with Holland. As part of the contract, trainloads of pipes run from the Corus plant at Hartlepool to Leith in Edinburgh to have anti-corrosive and concrete weighting coatings applied.

6S40, Hartlepool Pipe Works - Leith   6E40, Leith - Hartlepool Pipe Works

PETROLEUM PRODUCTS

EWS

a) After a few abortive attempts at the end of 2004, freight traffic finally restarts running over the former Preston Docks branch after a 10 year gap! The flow is Bitumen to a local terminal and the details are:

6M32, Lindsey - Preston Docks   6E32, Preston Docks - Lindsey

b) After a two year trial which saw both EWS and FHH jointly operate oil trains from Lindsey oil refinery to Kingsbury / Rectory Junction, petroleum giant TOTAL has opted for sole operation by EWS.

c) A new service starts this month between Lindsey and Spondon. It may well be a trial or the start of a regular flow - the last service to Spondon was the weekly train from Hull Saltend from Lindsey conveying Acetic Acid.

6Z28, Lindsey - Spondon   6Z29, Spondon - Lindsey

Both trains are booked to run via Lincoln and Nottingham.

GBRf

GBRf branch out into the petroleum sector by taking over the running of the Harwich - North Walsham condensate tanks (condensate being a bi-product from the North Sea Gas/Oil industry and reprocessed at the Harwich refinery) with timings unaltered. Later in the year, as we shall see, the Company will commence a long distance flow Harwich to Aberdeen.

GERRARDS CROSS STONE

(Above) : The terminal at Gerrards Cross receives stone from Acton Yard in conjunction with the construction of a new Tesco store. The train runs in top 'n' tail mode, as seen in February , with Class 59/2 No. 59203 *Vale of Pickering* nearest the camera on 7M36 and a rake of partially unloaded box wagons. (Fred Kerr, Feb-05)

EWS & MENDIP RAIL

(Bottom) : The new 10 year contract agreed by EWS and Mendip Rail, will mean more Mendip stone trains hauled by EWS locomotives. Class 60 No. 60052 *Glofa Twr* ... heads 7A09, Merehead - Acton past Shottesbrook Farm on March 26th and some 4,000 tonnes in tow! (Graham Lee)

WILLESDEN CEMENT

(Above Right) : The British Lime Industries new JGA tanks are seen behind Class 60 No. 60067 *James Clerk-Maxwell* heading 'down' the WCML near Dudswell on October 11th with 6H50, Willesden - Tunstead cement empties. (Anthony Kay)

NORTHENDEN STONE

(Below Right) : Class 60 No. 60022 stands in Northenden stone terminal, the site of the former Blue Circle cement terminal that closed after the opening of the newer Weaste terminal. Stone deliveries started with a 6H63, (WO) service from Dowlow and this October 15th view shows the class 60 shunting MEAs off a special working (6Z53) from Dowlow. Northenden Junction is visible in the distance, where the single (freight only) line leads to Hazel Grove H. L. Junction on the Stockport to Chinley main line.   (Alan Sherratt)

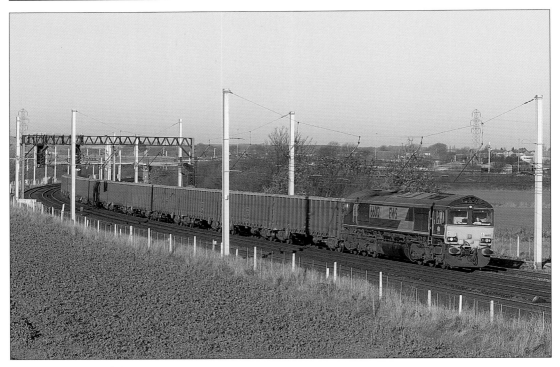

NORTHWICH FLYASH

(Above) : Initially, one train a day runs from Drax power station to Oakleigh Sidings conveying flyash for in-filling the old salt mines under Northwich. On one fine day in December, Class 66/0 No. 66012 heads loaded MBA wagons of flyash at Winwick, near Warrington, forming 6M27, Healey Mills - Northwich. (Fred Kerr)

(Below) : Class 60 No. 60028 is stabled at Oakleigh Sidings on May 26th with MBA empties bound for Healey Mills, alongside some new sparkling EWS liveried CTA tanks which will be used to remove brine as part of the stabilisation project under Northwich town centre; a project which should take five years to complete. (Chris Mills)

(Above) : Class 66/0 No. 66046 passes through Lostock Gralam station on February 17th with the empty MBAs from Oakleigh Sidings to Healey Mills. In the first few weeks of running, the return empties (6Z56) ran via Altrincham, Stockport and Denton before being rerouted via Warrington in both directions. (Alan Sherratt)

(Below) : A quick photograph and then a dash for cover when a cloud of flyash dust from the supposedly returning empties threatens to engulf the photographer as Class 66/0 No. 66241 speeds 6E56, Northwich - Healey Mills through Acton Bridge station on May 10th. (Joseph Gornall)

USKMOUTH COAL

(Above) : Class 66/0 No. 66090 comes off the Uskmouth branch with MGR empties on May 19th, following the resumption of coal services to Uskmouth (previously Fifoots) power station. (Chris Perkins)

LINCOLN SCRAP

(Below) : After a few trial runs, the 6G73, Lincoln - Healey Mills scrap starts running in earnest as Mainline branded Class 60 No. 60074 heads the train on May 19th past Saundby on the Lincoln to Doncaster mainline. On reaching Healey Mills, the wagons will go forward to Warrington and thence Liverpool Docks. (Chris Booth)

TUNSTEAD LIME

(Above) : A Wintry scene at Great Rocks on March 3rd as Class 66/5 No. 66524 slows for the junction and thence the single line to Tunstead Quarry with *FHH's* new 6Z55, Barrow Hill - Tunstead service, formed of a rake of 4-wheel hoppers used to convey lime to West Burton power station. Note the Class 60s in the background - a familiar sight which would attract a number of railway photographers to the Peak Forest area in 2005! (Ian Ball)

(Below) : A general view of the massive Tunstead quarry complex, photographed on July 11th. (Martin Buck)

EWS INTERMODALs

(Above) : Following the resumption of some EWS intermodal traffic in the new year after the threat of possible industrial action, Class 66/0 No. 66127 is seen arriving at Burton-on-Trent on August 31st with 4M78 from Southampton Western Docks; a dedicated container service for Argos. (Rich Norris)

(Below) : The introduction of a new Scottish intermodal (4D05, Inverness - Mossend) results in the regular sight of a class 66/67 pairing. On January 21st, Class 66/0 No. 66111 + Class 67 No. 67004 (DIT) haul 4D05, Inverness - Mossend past Allandale, which also includes the Lairg green-liveried oil tank empties. (Chris Perkins)

FORT WILLIAM ALUMINIUM TRAFFIC ....

(Above) : As a consequence of Freightliner losing the Fort William Aluminium ingot traffic to EWS, several freight changes take place. One is a new Coatbridge - Crewe freightliner (4M74) which is seen here on September 12th at Red Bank (Warrington) hauled by a pair of Class 86/6s Nos. 86620 *Philip G Walton* + 86609. Of note is that the leading locomotive caught fire some fifteen minutes after the photograph was taken! (Terry Eyres,)

(Below) : Additionally, EWS lay on an extra (Saturday) 'Enterprise' service between Mossend and Fort William in order to move freight over the West Highland Line six days a week. On August 11th, Class 66/0 No. 66110 passes County March summit, between Tyndrum and Bridge of Orchy, 6Y15, Mossend - Fort William 'Enterprise', comprising Alumina tanks and bogie bolster wagons. (Mark Bearton)

SPONDON TANKS

(Above) : After a lengthy absence, freight returns to Spondon in the shape of a new flow of petroleum from Lindsey oil refinery, Humberside. Seen adjacent to the Courtaulds Acetate factory at Spondon on March 14th, Class 66/0 No. 66057 proceeds slowly out of the sidings in order to join the main line with bogie tank wagons forming 6Z29, Spondon - Lindsey. (Ralf Edge)

NORTH WALSHAM 'BLUEBIRDS'

(Above) : On a glorious day in August, GBRf Class 66/7 No. 66711 make a fine sight crossing the River Stour viaduct at Manningtree, hauling 6A33, North Walsham - Harwich condensate tanks. (John Day)

(Below) : Meanwhile, the same train passes Lancaster Crossing, Stowmarket, on October 5th. with a rake of sixteen Carless bogie tanks in tow behind 'Bluebird' No. 66714 *Cromer Lifeboat*. (Nick Slocombe)

PRESTON DOCKS BITUMEN

(Above) : After a very stop/start affair, Bitumen tanks finally commence with a modicum of regularity to Preston Docks. Class 60 No. 60013 *Robert Boyle* passes the site of the old Lostock Hall steam shed on August 17th with 6E32, Preston Docks - Lindsey empty bogie tanks. (Mark Bearton)

(Below) : Meanwhile, Loadhaul-liveried Class 60 No. 60059 *Swinden Dalesman* passes Class 142 'Pacer' No. 142013 at Lostock Hall Junction with the 6E32, Preston Docks - Lindsey on August 15th. This train usually runs three times a week, departing Preston at 06:34, although for a short time last summer, due to a shortage of bogie tanks, the engine waited for the incoming tanks to be unloaded. So, by departing at 12:54, this allowed photographs of the train to be taken in the Preston area. (Mark Bearton)

FREIGHTMASTER

THE NATIONAL RAILFREIGHT TIMETABLE – 10TH ANNIVERSARY EDITION

Mark Rawlinson

No. 37
Spring
2005

AUTOMOTIVE

EWS

In gradual decline since the start of the year, the movement of cars from Sheerness / Queenborough to Bathgate (via Washwood Heath) has now ceased. However, there is a silver lining to this cloud, as a replacement service (6X52) is operating from Portbury to Washwood Heath, connecting into the overnight Washwood Heath to Bathgate train, which also conveys Peugeots from Bordersley to Bathgate.

CONSTRUCTION MATERIALS

EWS

Stone :

a) As stone traffic from South Wales continues to grow, EWS have won a new contract to move stone for Lafarge from Cardiff Docks to Kennett and utilises the rake of HGA hoppers used on the Jersey Marine to Thorney Mill / Angerstein circuit, which explains why the empties run from / to Margam:

6Z55, Margam - Cardiff Docks	6Z56, Cardiff Docks - Cardiff Tidal
6Z57, Cardiff Tidal - Kennett	6Z58, Kennett - Margam

b) Since the opening of the new stone terminal at West Drayton (on the site of of the old coal depot) last year, the only service has been a weekly Lafarge self-discharge train from Mountsorrel. This has now been joined by a twice-weekly ash train from West Thurrock:

6V23, West Thurrock - West Drayton	6M62, West Drayton - Wembley Yard

FHH

Freightliner *Heavy Haul* continue to expand their operating base out of Peak Forest, conveying lime for use in power station desulphurisation plants along with a new flow of stone to Hitchin using FHH box wagons:

Lime :

6Z51, Dowlow - Eggborough	6Z52, Eggborough - Dowlow
6Z85, Tunstead - Ratcliffe	6Z95, Ratcliffe - Tunstead
6Z35, Dowlow - Cottam	6Z36, Cottam - Dowlow

Stone :

6E99, Peak Forest - Hitchin	6Z58, Hitchin - Peak Forest

GBRf

Gypsum :

Following the installation of the flue-desulphurisation plant at West Burton Power Station, GBRf start running trains of Gypsum to Newbiggin; the first time the Company has worked timetabled services over the Settle & Carlisle:

4M52, West Burton - Newbiggin	4E16, Newbiggin - West Burton

DOMESTIC WASTE

FHH

a) As long ago as 2001, it was rumoured that Forders landfill site was becoming 'full', but some extra holes must have been found, because it has taken until now to finally run out of space. Since Monday 11th April, the daily 'binliner' from Cricklewood has been diverted to run to/from Calvert, initially on a trial basis:

6Z62, Cricklewood - Calvert   6Z51, Calvert - Cricklewood

Both trains are routed via West Hampstead (reverse), Dudding Hill, Acton Wells, Ealing Broadway, Greenford and High Wycombe.

b) As reported earlier, stone was being moved from Acton Yard to Gerrards Cross for tunnel construction work over the Chiltern main line, on top of which a new Tesco supermarket was being built. More than 300 steel-reinforced concrete arches were being erected to create the tunnel about 320 yards long, with a flat surface to support the store and car park

However, this work was suspended on 30 June when more than 50 yards of tunnel collapsed and tonnes of rubble spilled on to the line just before 8pm, causing disruption to Chiltern line services. One of the Chiltern Trains drivers, whose train was in Gerrards Cross station at the time, raised the alarm, and trains on the line between Marylebone station in London and Birmingham were immediately halted.

Consequently, this results in the diversion of two domestic waste trains to Calvert, from Cricklewood and Dagenham, via Ealing Broadway, Didcot and Oxford.

6M80, Dagenham - Calvert   6L81, Calvert - Dagenham
6Z62, Cricklewood - Calvert   6Z51, Calvert - Cricklewood

The line finally reopens to traffic on 22 August 2005.

INTERMODAL

DRS

Although the promised Knowsley to Wentloog service has fallen through, DRS have still managed to win some new intermodal traffic from the Merseyside area, this time in the shape of a daily containerised chemical train from Ditton to Purfleet:

4Z46, Ditton - Purfleet   4Z68, Purfleet - Ditton

The locomotives for this traffic are based at Crewe and run light to / from Ditton each morning and the new service commences Monday, 9th May 2005. The traffic has been created by a partnership between AHC (Warehousing) Ltd and Novatrans UK, one of the European leaders in combined transport, linking in with shipping into Purfleet operated by Cobelfret.

The Chairman of AHC (Warehousing) Ltd confirmed that the route was one of a number of new rail services planned for Widnes which is destined to become an important strategic area for rail freight movement.

METALS

EWS

a) Following the establishment of a new unloading siding on the site of Bristol East Depot yard, a new flow of steel sections has commenced:

6C01, Newport ADJ - Bristol East Depot   6C02, Bristol East Depot - Newport ADJ

The first train runs on Monday, 4th April, conveying steel sections from Teesside and Scunthorpe for onward delivery. The Bristol terminal, built on the site of the former Bristol East Down Sidings at a cost of £400,000, will receive a daily (weekdays) rail service forming part of the 'Enterprise' wagonload network.

b) After an 18 month absence, scrap metal traffic from Hamworthy to Cardiff has restarted, with the first train running on Friday 22nd April, running via Basingstoke and Didcot:

6Z47, Cardiff Tidal - Hamworthy Quay   6Z48, Hamworthy Quay - Cardiff Tidal

c) After a lengthy absence, EWS win another contract to move pipes from Hartlepool to Georgemas Junction, with a weekly train for 'several' months running as follows:

6X88, Hartlepool - Inverness   6X59, Inverness - Georgemas
6H57, Georgemas - Inverness   6E69, Inverness - Hartlepool

Both 6X88 and 6E69 are routed via Fife, so bringing regular freight traffic back to the Ladybank - Perth line.

LOGISTICS

EWS

After several years of operation in the northbound direction only, the nightly Walsall to Aberdeen 'express logistics' service now has a southbound counterpart:

1M07, 18:10 [SX] Aberdeen to Walsall

Apparently, after reaching Walsall, the vans are tripped to/from Bescot each night:

5M07, Walsall - Bescot Yard   5S03, Bescot Yard - Walsall

This new service replaces both 5D03 Aberdeen to Mossend and 1M02 Mossend to Walsall, with the result that the vans now remain at the Walsall end for 23 hours each day, with the class 67 being used on the Birch Coppice trip!

PETROLEUM PRODUCTS

GBRf

In addition to the North Walsham to Harwich tanks, GBRf's new contract with Carless also includes the movement of oil from Harwich to Aberdeen, which used to travel via Enterprise services, but will in future be conveyed by 'as required' block trains:

6S58, Harwich - Aberdeen   6L59, Aberdeen - Harwich

The first northbound train ran on Monday 18th April (a day late), with the loco returning light engine all the way back to Peterborough.

With the introduction of this new train, Aberdeen is now served by all four FOCs!

EWS

It is well over 12 months since Seal Sands last provided fuel oil to an Aire Valley power station (Ferrybridge) and the Teesside plant has now gained the contract to supply fuel oil to Eggborough power station, replacing the flow from Lindsey:

6D44, Seal Sands - Eggborough   6N36, Eggborough - Seal Sands

As with the previous flow, four-wheel tanks are employed instead of the more typical bogie tanks used on these flows.

S. & C. GYPSUM

(Above) : Following a successful Saturday service, GBRf start running weekday gypsum trains between West Burton power station and Newbiggin. On the approach to Appleby station, Class 66/7 No. 66706 *Nene Valley* passes two fine examples of semaphore signalling while working 4M52, West Burton - Newbiggin. (Fred Kerr)

Below) : Passing Garsdale on June 28th, Class 66/7 No. 66713 *Forest City* heads south with empty gypsum containers forming 4E16, Newbiggin - West Burton. (Robert Armitstead)

BIRCH COPPICE 'TRIP'

Following the introduction of the new southbound logistics train from Motherwell to Walsall (1M07), EWS have ensured work for the 'booked' class 67 locomotive during its layover before working back north on the corresponding logistics service.

The locomotive is diagrammed to work the Birch Coppice 'trip' from Bescot and two views of the service are shown on this page.

(Right) :On the approach to Water Orton station, Class 67 No. 67011 heads along the 'up fast' Birmingham to Derby main line on a fine July morning with 6G36, Bescot - Birch Coppice 'Enterprise'.

The tracks on the left serve Nuneaton, with the nearest line doubling up as the 'down fast' from Derby and the 'up fast' to Nuneaton. (Martin Buck)

(Below) : On the Birch Coppice branch itself, Class 67 No. 67002 *Special Delivery* is seen in the cutting at Kingsbury Link 0n June 8th with the returning 6G42 'trip' to Bescot. (Peter Tandy)

FHH EXPANSION ....

Freightliner *Heavy Haul* continue to expand their aggregate flows out of Peak Forest, especially trains of limestone to delsurphurisation plants at Airedale and East Midlands power stations.

(Above Left) : This evocative view shot on September 20th shows Class 66/6 No. 66601 *The Hope Valley* passing three class 60s stabled at Peak Forest with a mixed rake of loaded hoppers forming 6Z85, the 11:50 Tunstead - Ratcliffe. (Chris Perkins)

(Below Left) : With the eight cooling towers of Eggborough power station dominating the background, Class 66/5 No. 66547 passes High Eggborough on April 29th with a consist of 4-wheel + *FHH* hoppers, forming 6Z52, the 15:00 Eggborough - Dowlow limestone empties. (Ian Ball)

(Above Right) : Another view of 6Z85, this time on July 12th on the northern approach to Chesterfield station, with Class 66/6 No. 66612 having crossed over onto the 'up goods' line at Tapton Junction. (Martin Buck)

(Below) : On September 20th, mounds of aggregate from Dove Holes quarry tower over Class 66/5 No. 66558, and three of the distinctive *FHH* green liveried box wagons, which have just arrived on 6Z58, the 10:08 Hitchin - Peak Forest. (Chris Perkins)

GBRf 'MUD OIL'

(Above) : Probably the 'new freight flow of the year' and a most welcome addition to freight services in Scotland, the transportation of drilling oil in TTA wagons from Harwich to Aberdeen. Sometimes, the train locomotive will run light engine' from the GBRf depot at Peterborough to Aberdeen! On October 23rd, Class 66/7 No. 66714 *Cromer Lifeboat* passes Mistley, running on this occasion as 6E60, Harwich - Peterborough. (Iain Scotchman)

(Below) : Class 66/7 No. 66708 passes Ferryhill at the outset of a long journey south on July 8th for 6L59, Aberdeen - Harwich, having just crossed the River Dee. (Guy Houston)

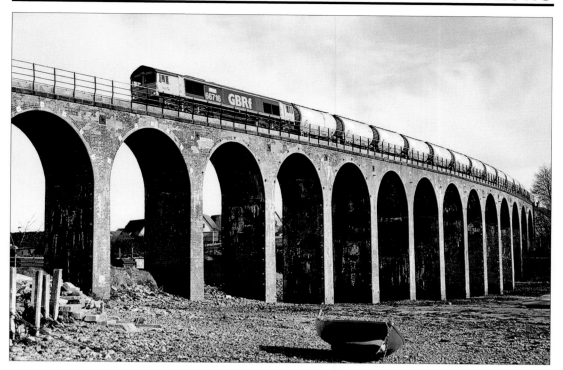

(Above) : Class 66/7 No. 66716 *Willesden Traincare Centre* on Rossie Viaduct, Montrose, with the inaugural run of 6L59, Aberdeen - Harwich on April 19th. The inward service was originally coded 6S58, but later changed to 6S60 to avoid conflict with 6S58, Lackenby - Dalzell steel that ran a few hours ahead of the tanks. (Guy Houston)

(Below) :Another bridge scene, but this time the use of a telephoto lens helps to capture Class 66/7 No. 66708 on camera heading away from Dundee crossing the Tay Bridge on July 8th with 6L59; this, along with the Grangemouth - Linkswood tanks and Aberdeen - Oxwellmains empty cement, being the only freight the Tay Bridge currently sees. (Jim Ramsay)

BRISTOL STEEL

(Above) : An elevated view shows the new Bristol steel terminal, located adjacent to the Great Western Main Line on the site of the former Bristol East Depot civil engineers sidings. The terminal officially opens on 4th April and will result in 2.1 million lorry miles being saved each year between Bristol and Teesside! (Martin Buck)

(Below) : The terminal receives steel from Teesside using a dedicated 'Enterprise' working (6C01, Newport Alexandra Dock Junction - Bristol East Depot), like the one run on April 22nd, when Class 60 No. 60032 *William Booth* could be seen shunting bogie bolster wagons laden with steel. (John Chalcraft)

NEW DRS INTERMODAL

(Above) : On the first day of service, May 9th, Class 66/4 No. 66407 crosses onto the 'up slow' line at Tamworth Low Level with 4Z46, the 12:05 Ditton - Purfleet intermodal. The payload on this occasion being several more tanks of chemicals than the train will normally be seen to carry! (Martin Buck)

(Below) : On the same day, 4Z46 is seen further into its journey at Upper Holloway on the seldom photographed Gospel Oak - South Tottenham line. (Nick Slocombe)

SEAL SANDS OIL

(Above) : EWS-liveried Class 60 No. 60096 comes off the Eggborough branch onto the Knottingley to Goole main line at Whitley Bridge with a rake of empty 4-wheel tank wagons on May 6th, forming 6N36, Eggborough - Seal Sands; Eggborough power station can be seen in the background. (Ian Ball)

SANDBACH ACID TANKS

(Below) : On the balmy Summer evening of June 10th, a DRS Class 20 / Class 37 pairing of Nos. 20308 and 37259 pass Ravenglass on the Cumbrian Coast Line with 6P27, Sandbach - Sellafield loaded Sulphuric Acid tanks; a train that had not run for some time due to problems at Sellafield, hence the five-tank load. (Kevin Smith)

COAL

FHH

Following the refettling of the line down to Ellesmere Port in July, FHH have commenced running two trains a day to Fiddlers Ferry Power Station:

	4F02, Garston - Ellesmere Port
6F02, Ellesmere Port - Fiddlers Ferry	4F03, Fiddlers Ferry - Ellesmere Port
6F03, Ellesmere Port - Fiddlers Ferry	4F04, Fiddlers Ferry - Garston

EWS

a) Hot on the heals of FHH, another new imported coal flow starts running to Fiddlers Ferry, this time from Portbury and operated by EWS:

	4V09, Washwood Heath - Portbury Dock
6M02, Portbury Dock - Fiddlers Ferry	4G20, Fiddlers Ferry - Washwood Heath
and,	
	4V17, Washwood Heath - Portbury Dock
6M12, Portbury Dock - Fiddlers Ferry	4G22, Fiddlers Ferry - Washwood Heath

b) EWS conduct three days of trials in September on the West Coast Main Line utilising a Class 92 locomotive and an extended rake of EWS coal hoppers, with the aim of extracting more work from the under-utilised Class 92s and speedier journey times for WCML coal traffic.

The trial which takes place on 20 September utilises EWS-liveried Class 92 No. 92001 *Victor Hugo* powering 6M04, the 08:55 Hunterston - Fiddlers Ferry with Class 66/0 No. 66090 provided inside due to the 92's coupling incompatibility with the hoppers.

ENTERPRISE

EWS

a) A major reorganisation by StoraEnso of its supply chain sees the end of paper imports via Felixstowe and the Channel Tunnel, both being replaced by a new facility at Tilbury. Sadly, a consequence is the loss of the well known Ripple Lane traffic, which latterly ran from Dollands Moor and before that Immingham. However, EWS has managed to gain flows from Tilbury to Selby and Avonmouth via the 'Enterprise'.

6L01, Wembley - Tilbury	6M81, Tilbury - Wembley

b) Due to the demise of the paper traffic from Felixstowe, the nightly Harwich to Wembley Enterprise has been withdrawn, with the Saturday fuel oil tranks to Ipswich running as a dedicated train to/from Wembley:

6L00, Wembley - Ipswich yard	6M00, Ipswich yard - Wembley

ENTERPRISE *(continued)*

c) Ridham Dock, between Sittingbourne and Sheerness, enters the 'Enterprise' network with EWS moving goods there from Germany, via the Channel Tunnel. The traffic runs as far as Hoo Junction on existing 'Enterprise' services and is then 'tripped' to Ridham, thus:

6U79, Hoo Junction - Ridham Dock - Queenborough
6U80, Queenborough - Hoo Junction

This flow will eliminate 1,200 lorry journeys and the first train runs on 23 August, hauled by Class 66/0 Locomotive No. 66151.

EUROPEAN

EWS

EWS send Class 66/0 No. 66083 to France in order to get the class certified for operation on the Continent. The class 66 was towed through the Channel Tunnel by a class 92 locomotive, returning to the UK three days later. The visit is part of an approval procedure by EWS to have its locos. accepted for operation in France by its subsidiary, Euro Cargo Rail (ECR): a safety certificate being granted by the French Minister of Transport later in the month.

FREIGHTLINER

FHH

a) Remember the Tilbury to Swindon 'Butterliner' - a Freightliner block train which used to convey imported Anchor butter ...

... well, August sees a similar type of operation commence, this time conveying imported Canadian beans from Thamesport to Ely for Crosse and Blackwell.

The train runs weekly, via Hitchin, as follows:

4Z86, Thamesport - Ely Papworths   4Z87, Ely Papworths - Thamesport

b) Until mid-September, container traffic between Coatbridge/Leeds and Thamesport was all routed via Tilbury, and 'tripped' on a morning service between Tilbury and Thamesport. This 'shuttle' has now been withdrawn, and replaced by an unusual triangular service:

4E24, Thamesport   - Leeds Stourton (via ECML)
4M24, Leeds Stourton   - Crewe Basford Hall
4O86, Crewe Basford Hall - Thamesport

INTERMODAL

EWS

Due to congestion in the Greater London area, EWS re-activate the mothballed Willesden Euroterminal and introduce a new nightly service to Thamesport:

6O86, Willesden - Thamesport   6M10, Thamesport - Willesden

CONSTRUCTION MATERIALS

EWS

Brine :

After several months delay, the Northwich brine trains finally start running, initially as:

6F26, Oakleigh Sidings - Middlewich   6F27, Middlewich - Oakleigh Sidings

The brine is pumped out from the old salt mines and transferred in CTA bogie tank wagons to the salt works at Middlewich for processing. The mines are then in-filled with flyash from Drax.

China Clay :

A long-standing flow stops running on Monday, 11 July; the Mondays Only china clay train from Plymouth to Dollands Moor for export, reporting number:

6O92, Tavistock Junction - Dollands Moor

FHH

Freightliner *Heavy Haul* continue to expand their share of the aggregate market this Summer ....

Stone :

a) FHH start yet another new (weekly) flow out of Dove Holes Quarry, Peak Forest, this time serving Attercliffe Road, Sheffield. The train uses the same wagons as the Hitchin service, so running days may vary. Due to layout restrictions at Attercliffe Road, the loaded train has to approach it's destination from the north, which is achieved by running first to Doncaster decoy Yard, where a run-round takes place:

6Z99, Peak Forest - Attercliffe Road   6Z57, Attercliffe Road - Peak Forest

b) After a short trial period, FHH take over the operation of the weekly Lafarge stone trains from Dowlow to Kennett and Barham, which now runs as follows:

6Z20, Dowlow - Barham   6Z19, Barham - Dowlow
6Z20, Dowlow - Kennett   6Z19, Kennett - Dowlow

On Thursdays and/or Fridays, the wagons are used on lime trips to Cottam/Eggborough power stations. Following this development, FHH now operate well over half of all freight trains through the Hope Valley - an amazing achievement, from a starting point of nothing!

GBRf

Gypsum :

After a lengthy absence, the flow of Gypsum starts running again between Southampton Western Docks and Mountfield:

4Y81, Southampton W.D. - Mountfield   4Y19, Mountfield - Southampton W.D

METALS

EWS

After seeing no traffic for a couple of years, pipe trains are once again running from Stanton Gate, just north of Toton, to Tees Dock:

6Z71, Stanton Gate - Tees Yard

6P10, Toton - Stanton Gate

6Z91, Tees Yard - Toton

The pipes are tripped between Tees Yard and Tees Dock.

PETROLEUM PRODUCTS

EWS

a) The only main line not to see regular freight traffic since the end of steam is the Portsmouth direct line from Guildford to Havant via Petersfield. However, this has now changed due to the re-routing of the crude oil train from Holybourne, which now runs this way to avoid a run-round at Woking.

The thrice-weekly train now runs as follows:

6Y30, Fawley - Holybourne (via Hamble)   6Y31, Holybourne - Eastleigh (via Botley)

b) Just like the Dollands Moor china clay working, another familiar sight disappears for good from the Summer timetable - the flow of Liquefied Petroleum Gas (LPG) from the BP plant at Furzebrook to Avonmouth, conveyed in distinctive white liveried with orange band four wheel tank wagons.

ELLESMERE PORT COAL

(Above) : It is pleasing to report the resumption of freight traffic to Ellesmere Port in the shape of *FHH* coal trains to Fiddlers Ferry power station. On August 8th, Class 66/6 No. 66616   passes Ince & Elton, between Stanlow and Helsby, with 6F02, the 12:13 Ellesmere Port - Fiddlers Ferry. (Geoff Morris)

(Below) : On August 12th, the same loco. as above, receives the road to Ellesmere Port at Helsby with 4F03, the 15:15 Fiddlers Ferry - Ellesmere Port empty hoppers. (Geoff Morris)

(Above) : Fiddlers Ferry power station is in view, as Class 66/6 No. 66608 passes Fiddlers Ferry Marina running a tadge early at 07:30hrs on September 3rd with 4F02, the 07:37 Garston - Ellesmere Port empties. (Ian Ball)

(Below) : All coal trains to Fiddlers Ferry power station gain access via Warrington and a run-round in Latchford Sidings as evidenced in this August 3rd view of Class 66/6 No. 66616 departing from the sidings with 6F02, the 12:13 Ellesmere Port - Fiddlers Ferry loaded hopper wagons. (Alan Sherratt)

IPSWICH FUEL OIL

(Above) : The Ipswich fuel oil tanks now run direct from Wembley and the returning empty tanks are seen at Witham on September 17th with Class 66/0 No. 66156 in charge of 6M00, (Sat) Ipswich Yard - Wembley. (Iain Scotchman)

GBRf GYPSUM

(Above Left) : As one flow restarts another stops .... the Southampton Western Docks - Mountfield gypsum recommences. In glorious warm Autumn weather, Class 66/7 No. 66715 *Valour* .... powers 4Y15, Mountfield - Southampton Western Docks empty containers through Addlestone on October 10th. (Chris Nevard)

(Below Left) : Meanwhile, the West Burton - Mountfield flow ceases and with it a familiar sight, such as Class 66/7 No. 66705 *Golden Jubilee* ambling along the ECML near Langford on March 18th with 4E19, the returning gypsum empties to West Burton power station. (Anthony Kay)

STANTON GATE PIPES

(Below) : The loaded Stanton Gate pipes is an impressive sight as Class 66/0 No. 66135 passes Radskelf, near Northallerton, on November 10th, hauling a massive 6E77, Stanton Gate - Tees Dock. (Rich Norris)

FHH EAST ANGLIAN STONE

(Above) : *FHH* venture into East Anglia by taking over the flows of limestone on behalf of Lafarge to terminals at Barham and Kennett and on July 16th, Class 66/6 No. 66614 passes Manea with 6L20, Dowlow - Barham loaded limestone using a combination of 4-wheel wagons and HHAs. (Ian Ball)

(Above Left) : Class 66/5 No. 66564 crosses the Twenty Foot Drain, near Turves, on October 25th with 6Z19, Barham - Dowlow limestone empties. (John Rudd)

(Below Left) : If provenance was needed then the McCain's factory at Kings Dyke, near Peterborough, certainly provides it as No. 66619 passes with the returning 6Z19 empties to Dowlow on July 12th. (John Rudd)

(Below) : Apologies for the apparent 6Z19 overkill, but this service does offer great photographic opportunities in East Anglia, especially at one of the top photographic locations in the country. No. 66531 passes the magnificent cathedral at Ely on November 1st with the returning limestone empties to Dowlow. (John Rudd)

FREIGHT CASUALTIES

China Clay : : Unfortunately, the year in question sees the end of two long established flows; the first being the Mondays-only Dollands Moor china clay service, effective 11th July. In happier times, Class 66/0 No. 66054 *(Above)* accelerates up the grade near Wellington three weeks earlier (June 20th to be precise) with 6092, Tavistock Junction - Dollands Moor. (Pete Slater)

LPG : Meanwhile, the axe falls on the LPG (Liquefied Petroleum Gas) flow from the British Petroleum plant at Furzebrook to Hallen Marsh, Avonmouth. The train was easily identified by the white 4-wheel tanks with orange band as Class 66/0 No. 66029 *(Below)* approaches Eastleigh on April 28th with a rake of the empty tanks on a much delayed 6O10, Hallen Marsh - Eastleigh Yard. (Chris Nevard)

FREIGHTMASTER

THE NATIONAL RAILFREIGHT TIMETABLE

No. 39
Autumn
2005

Mark Rawlinson

STOCK MOVEMENTS

During recent years, EWS, GBRf and Freightliner have all been involved in moving withdrawn ex-Southern Region 'Slam Door' EMUs to disposal sites for scrapping, a practice which will continue in the immediate future.

With this in mind, it is worth mentioning a landmark event which occurred on 7 October when the last 'slam door' working by South Eastern Trains took place: EMU set 3565+3545+3568 worked the 06:38 Ashford - Cannon Street and 18:04 Cannon Street - Ashford; thence e.c.s. to Ramsgate. From there, Class 66/7 No. 66713 hauls the set on the 27th. to MoD Pig's bay, Shoeburyness.

The only 'Slam Door' EMUs to remain in service are two sets for the Lymington branch.

Typical scrap movement trains (or 'Scrappers', as they are referred to) are by way of example:

  Timetabled Service   : 6V91, Shoeburyness - Newport Docks

  Special Train Plan   : 5Z23, Ramsgate   - Immingham

                             5Z41, Ramsgate   - Caerwent

PETROLEUM PRODUCTS

EWS

On the 14/15 October, EWS run a class 60-hauled test from Robeston Refinery (near Milford Haven) to Westerleigh with 30 loaded MURCO TEA bogie tanks, instead of the usual 24/25.

ENTERPRISE

EWS

Since the cessation of coke traffic from Humber, there has been no railfreight traffic to Holyhead, but now EWS has gained some new business from Holy Island conveying aluminium products in Cargowagons, bound for Germany via the Channel Tunnel.

The train is powered by a class 66, although both 60s and 67s will also put in an appearance:

  6J00, Warrington Arpley - Holyhead   6F00, Holyhead - Warrington

6V91

(Above Right) : This working gives photographers their only opportunity to photograph GBRf 'Bluebirds' working timetabled services on the Great Western Main Line. Class 66/7 No. 66717 nears journey's end on July 19th as it hauls withdrawn EMU stock through Newport with 6V91, Shoeburyness - Newport Docks. (John Chalcraft)

MURCO TRIAL

(Below Right) : A pair of Class 60's were used for an (overnight) load test between Robeston and Westerleigh. The normal service having been increased by 5 x 100 Tonne wagons to give a trailing load of 3,150 Tonnes, the second loco. (while manned) was provided as security in case of difficulty. The return working was booked as the 11:18, Westerleigh - Robeston which is seen approaching Wickwar Tunnel on October 15th behind 60036 *GEFCO* + 60085 *MINI Pride of Oxford*, only the lead engine under power. (John Chalcraft)

DIVERSIONS

S. & C.

(Above) : When the WCML is closed between Carlisle and Preston due to engineering work or in the case of emergencies, services are invariably diverted over the spectacular Settle & Carlisle. Such was the case on March 12th, when Class 66/0 No. 66141 was filmed high on Ribblehead Viaduct, heading 6S55, Burngullow - Irvine china clay tanks; freight is regularly diverted during Spring as a result of WCML upgrade work. (Robert Armitstead)

(Below) : For three weekends in March, the ECML was closed in the Durham/Tyneside area for engineering work. As a result, 6M46, Redcar - Hardendale lime train was diverted via the S. & C. on March 19th and Mainline-liveried Class 60 No. 60044 seen catching the last rays of sunshine at Selside with 6M46. (Robert Armitstead)

ANDOVER 'SCRAPPER'

(Above) : The majority of 'Scrappers' for disposal in South Wales go via Reading and Swindon. However, due to an 'incident' near Didcot on April 14th, 5Z23, the 12:32 Wimbledon - Caerwent was unusually routed via Andover/Salisbury and unbranded Freightliner loco. Class 47/8 No. 47830 is seen hauling the train (EMUs 3405 and 3456) crossing Hurstbourne Viaduct to the east of Andover. As a rule, the only freight to use this route are MoD specials to Ludgershall. (Kevin Smith)

6O92

(Below) : Normally, the (MO) Tavistock Junction - Dollands Moor china clay working is routed via the 'Berks. & Hants.' but due to engineering work on March 28th, the train was routed via Swindon; Class 66/0 No. 66073 is seen on 6O92 passing Uffington, about midway between Swindon and Didcot. (Kevin Smith)

DIVERSIONS

PATCHWAY BLOCKADES

During April, services to/from South Wales using Severn Tunnel were diverted via Gloucester and Chepstow due to engineering work in Patchway Tunnel; presenting photographers with excellent photographic opportunities.

(Above) : At Stonehouse on April 14th, Class 60 No. 60088 *Buachaille Etive Mor* is about to join the Bristol - Birmingham main line off the Swindon branch with 6V60, Angerstein - Margam. (Rich Norris)

(Above Right) : Looking across the Severn estuary at Purton (near Lydney) on April 5th, there was the unusual sight of Class 59/2 No. 59204 *Vale of Glamorgan* on a rake of Hanson hoppers, returning to South Wales with 6B84, Westbury - Machen stone empties. (Pete Slater)

(Below Right) : Skirting the coastline at Gatcombe on the Chepstow main line, Class 66/5 No.66503 heads the diverted 4O51, Cardiff Wentloog - Millbrook freightliner on April 18th, passing Class 170 unit No. 170502 on a Nottingham - Cardiff Central service in the process. (Pete Slater)

(Below) : Looking in the opposite direction to the view above, Class 66/0 No. 66073 prepares to join the Swindon line at Standish Junction with 6M17, Newport ADJ- Wembley 'Enterprise'. (Rich Norris, 21-Apr-05)

DIVERSIONS

CIRCUITOUS ROUTES

(Above) : The Burngullow - Irvine (6S55) china clay slurry tanks followed a very unusual route on September 24th when Class 66/0 No. 66082 hauled the service via Toton, Erewash Valley, York and Newcastle, thence Carlisle and, presumably, the G & SW route. Blockages between Shrewsbury and Crewe, Crewe and Carlisle were to blame and the train is seen passing Stenson. (Rich Norris)

(Below) : Due to a blockage between Gloucester and Worcester, North/South services were diverted via Oxford and Swindon or Shrewsbury on September 9th. This provided the rare opportunity to see freight traffic on the Shrewsbury - Wolverhampton main line, such as Class 66/0 No. 66025 passing Upton Magna with the diverted 6M41, (Sun) Margam - Round Oak steel service. (Rich Norris)

WCML

(Above) : When engineering work occurs in the Trent Valley, WCML freight services are usually diverted via Bescot, but on November 4th, Class 90 No. 90016 + Class 57 No. 57012 *Freightliner Envoy* are seen passing Sandwell Valley Park between Wolverhampton and Birmingham on 4L97, Trafford Park - Ipswich freightliner. (Rich Norris)

(Below) : Weekend engineering work on the southern stretch of the WCML resulted in some freights being diverted via the Chiltern Line, with the majority routed via Reading, Didcot and Banbury. Class 66/7 No. 66717 approaches Banbury on March 12th with 4M21, Hams Hall - Felixstowe intermodal. (Peter Tandy)

DIVERSIONS

BATHGATE CARTICS

(Above) : Class 66/0 No. 66088 heads 6Z85, the 13:39 Bathgate - Carlisle empty car transporters north of Lockerbie on October 8th. Unusual to find this on the WCML as it normally runs as 6M85, Bathgate - Washwood Heath via the ECML to Doncaster where it splits for Washwood Heath and Portbury, but on this particular weekend the ECML was closed. (Tom Noble)

BARRHEAD TANKS

(Below) : Supposedly, the first time in 10 years a Class 60 has been seen at Barrhead as No. 60011 heads 6D61, Riccarton - Mossend empty bogie tanks through the station on November 22nd. The train was originally routed via Dalry and it remains to be seen how long 6D61 will be routed via Barrhead. (Guy Houston)

SOUTH COAST 'LINERS

(Above) : Class 66/5 No. 66541 approaches the former Ashbury Crossing near Shrivenham on March 25th with 4O54, Leeds - Southampton; freightliners being diverted to/from the south coast via Swindon and Westbury to avoid Easter weekend engineering work in the Reading and Basingstoke areas. (Kevin Smith)

SHIELDMUIR MAIL

(Below) : The GBRf operated mail trains are usually seen running up and down the WCML, sometimes hauled by a Class 87 locomotive when a Class 325 mail unit is found to be defective. Here, the somewhat unusual sight of Class 87 No. 87012 *Coeur de Lion* (resplendent in Network South East livery) on the ECML passing Burn on December 10th with 1Z97, the 06:31 Shieldmuir - Willesden PRDC Christmas additional mail service. The Class 325 units in tow are Nos. 325015/001/005. (Alan Sherratt)

CALVERT 'BINS'

(Above) : As a result of the Chiltern Line closure at Gerrards Cross following the tunnel collapse, 'Binliners' from Dagenham (6M80 / 6L81) and Northolt (6A55 / 6A56) to Calvert were diverted via Reading, Didcot and Oxford. The loaded 'binliner' from Dagenham (6M80) is seen on July 14th in a cutting on the Great Western Main Line at Purley-on-Thames hauled by Class 66/6 No. 66609. (Martin Buck)

WHEN THE BOAT COMES IN ....

(Above) : During the first few months of 2005, supplies of imported gypsum were shipped into Southampton Western Docks and moved by rail to Newbiggin, with special trains running until the ship's hold had been emptied! This presented the unusual sight of gypsum traffic on Great Western metals, such as on February 8th when Class 60 No. 60099 *Ben More Assynt* passed Manor Farm, Cholsey, with 6Z87, the 07:58 Milford Sidings - Southampton Western Docks gypsum empties. (Kevin Lee)

DRS 'WEDDING EX'

(Below) : DRS Class 37/6 locomotives Nos. 37609 and 37606 top 'n' tailed a one off working using the Queen of Scots stock on April 2nd, forming 1Z37, the 15:00 Crewe - Crewe via Chester and Shrewsbury for the marriage of Tony Mosley, LNWR's Managing Director. The train is seen at Hargrave near Chester. (Alan Sherratt)

FREIGHT LOCOS. ON TOUR

It is a common sight, railfreight locomotives working charter trains for rail enthusiasts over rare track around the UK rail network and a brief sample for 2005 is included here.

(Above) : Freightliner's Class 66/6 No. 66608 is seen on May 30th coming off the Heysham branch at Morecambe with a Pathfinder Tours special train from Reading to Heysham Harbour. (Fred Kerr)

(Opposite) : An imposing sight, as onlookers witness Class 66/0 No. 66103 on June 25th crossing the swing bridge, which gives access to the marina at Preston Docks, with an Ealing Broadway - Preston Docks charter. (Fred Kerr)

(Below) : A pleasant rural scene as GBRF Class 73's Nos. 73204 *Janice* & 73209 *Alison* double head the 15:05 Minehead - Bishops Lydeard West Somerset Railway Diesel Gala service at Nethercott on May 8th; No. 73205 *Jeanette* was at the rear. (John Chalcraft)

MOSSEND MARAUDER

(Above) : In less than perfect weather conditions on June 2nd, Class 66/6 No. 66622, complete with *Mossend Marauder* headboard, passes Carnoustie with 6Y40, the 05:10 Huntly - Millerhill empty ballast hoppers. This was Freightliner's first non-cement traffic north of the central belt in Scotland - until then all permanent way trains had been in the hands of EWS. (Jim Ramsay)

(Left) : The same train is seen for a second time passing through Montrose station. (Guy Houston)

'G8' MAIL

(Above Right) : GBRf, on behalf of Royal Mail, ran a 'one-off' (1Z95) Shieldmuir - Aberdeen additional mail service in reaction to possible road disruption caused by the G8 Conference at Gleneagles. Cotswold Rail Class 47 No. 47200 *The Fosse Way* is seen at West Ferry on July 6th with Class 325 unit No. 325005 (a first for Aberdeen!) on 1Z96, the 11:30 Aberdeen - Shieldmuir mail. (Jim Ramsay

(Below Right) : On the same day, No. 47200 awaits departure at Aberdeen with 1Z96, which actually ran empty, although 1Z95 did carry mail. (Guy Houston)

MoD SPECIALS

(Above) : EWS are responsible for transporting military goods and hardware for the Ministry of Defence; some trains running under the 'Enterprise' network and others as 'one-off' specials. Seen passing Golf Street, Carnoustie, on August 1st , Class 67 No. 67007 heads 6Z83, Montrose - Mossend MoD vehicles from RM Condor, Arbroath. The train originates from Montrose as existing facilities at Arbroath are not suitable for this traffic. (Jim Ramsay)

(Below) : Class 66/0 No. 66149 is stabled at Rosyth Dockyard on November 21st in readiness to depart with 6Z20, the 10:20 Rosyth - Mossend (to Devonport) flask wagon, a move in conjunction with the switch by the Royal Navy of nuclear refurbishments from Rosyth to Devonport. (Guy Houston)

CAMBRIAN SOJOURN

(Above) : Freights, of any description, are not commonplace on Cambrian metals and Class 37/4 No. 37405 enjoyed a rare outing over the route on October 15th when entrusted to work an engineers train from Crewe to Pwllheli. The returning ensemble, running as 6W31, Pwllheli - Crewe, is seen on the single line at Hook-a-Gate, near Shrewsbury. (Rich Norris)

6M16

(Below) : An unusual and unique sight greeted the cameraman on July 14th when Class 66/6 No. 66621 appeared at Purley-on-Thames hauling 6M16, Southampton Western Docks - Crewe car/van train complete with a loaded *FHH* coal hopper at the front of the consist. Apparently, the 'crippled' wagon off a Hunterston - Ferrybridge working should have been removed at Crewe from an overnight service from Mossend, but was 'overlooked', hence the round trip to Southampton! (Martin Buck)

SPECIALS

FORSINARD CWR

(Left) : During September, at least two trains of Continuous Welded Rails (CWR) ran to the Far North Line as 6Y25, Millerhill - Forsinard, hauled by Freightliner locomotives.

As seems to be the case when something special runs in Scotland, the weather closes in and the light is far from ideal for taking photographs. On a dismal October 4th Class 66/5 No. 66526 heads 6Y25 away from Perth during its 300-mile journey. (Guy Houston)

LEITH COAL

(Middle) : Branch line freight always attracts the attention of railway photographers, such as when MGR coal services resumed running out of Leith Docks, Edinburgh.

Class 66/0 No. 66067 prepares to leave the docks on August 5th with 7B01, Leith Docks - Cockenzie power station. (Iain Scotchman)

(Below) : Meanwhile, on the branch itself, No. 66067 makes its way with 7B01 towards Portobello Junction, where it will join the ECML for the short run to Prestonpans, thence down the branch to Cockenzie power station. (Iain Scotchman)

DRS 'HI-CUBES'

(Above) : This particular working caused much confusion in the railway press, when a new DRS intermodal service had been reported as running between Swindon and Carlisle. Alas, this was not the case, simply a DRS pairing of Nos. 20308+37218 taking redundant Hi-Cube wagons off the Swindon - Longbridge circuit to Carlisle. The train ran on May 25th as 4Z56 and is seen here at Lower Hatton on the WCML. (Rich Norris)

325s On the GWML

(Below) : Possibly the first sighting of a Class 325 EMU at Oldfield Park! On December 2nd, Class 47/8 No. 47840 *North Star* heads Class 325 units Nos. 325009 and 325015 (plus Class 57/6 No. 57602 at the rear) on the return test working (5Z37) from Bristol Parkway RMT to Willesden RDC. (John Chalcraft)

DRS 33s

(Above) : DRS declare the Class 33 locomotives to be 'sub-standard' and trains would be hauled by Class 20, 37 and 66/4 locomotives. As a result, scenes such as these two illustrations will be confined to the history books. Running alongside the beautiful Cumbrian coast on June 7th, No. 33030 passes Seascale Banks with 7C20, Sellafield - Drigg low level waste. (Kevin Smith)

(Below) : The DRS 33s were generally under-used though 6C52, Sellafield - Heysham flasks was a regular working for the class. On June 14th, No. 33207 had failed in the Dalton area and was propelled into Carnforth station by sister locomotive No. 33029. (Mark Bearton)

DRS 37s

(Above) : During January, the DRS Class 66/4 fleet was sidelined due to brake problems and pairs of Class 37s took over their duties. On the WCML, passing Heamies Farm near Norton Bridge on January 21st, No. 37029 heads another unidentified 37 on 4M44, Mossend - Daventry. (Chris Perkins)

37402 *'Bont Y Bermo'*

(Below) : The movement of 'celebrity' locomotives is closely followed by enthusiasts, especially when Class 37s are involved. On January 25th, a resplendent No. 37402 + No. 37669 double-head 6G42, Birch Coppice - Bescot 'Enterprise' seen passing Lea Marston, which can also be routed via Whitacre Junction. (Peter Tandy)

EDINBURGH 'BINS'

(Above) : The Edinburgh 'Bins' was the only timetabled freight service to be officially 'diagrammed' a Class 37 in 2005. Heading along the 'Down Berwick' of the ECML at Prestonpans on August 5th, No. 37406 *The Saltire Society* is seen in charge of 6B44, Oxwellmains – Powderhall empty binliner. (Iain Scotchman)

37411

(Below) : Class 37/4 No. 37411 *The Scottish Railway Preservation Society* passes Raskelf on April 18th with 6E09, Margam - Lackenby steel empties; a move to get 37411 to Toton for painting in green livery. (Ian Ball)

57302 'Virgil Tracy'

(Above) : It is a fairly rare event for a Class 57/3 'Thunderbird' to haul a freight train, but one did take place on April 24th when Class 37 No. 37422 *Cardiff Canton* failed on 6K50, Toton - Crewe Basford Hall engineers train and was rescued by No. 57302 . The ensemble is seen passing Lichfield. (Rich Norris)

EWS 'STICKERS'

EWS still retains many locomotives in their fleet which do not carry the red & yellow corporate livery. So, perhaps in an attempt to save money on repainting, the freight Company have started to apply stickers bearing the EWS Co. logo to the sides of locomotives still in Loadhaul, Mainline and Transrail liveries.

(Middle) : A new sticker, which depicts the EWS logo comprising an English lion, Welsh dragon and Scottish stag is clearly visible on the bodyside of Mainline Blue Class 60 No. 60078 seen leaving Bath on October 25th with 6B66, Westbury Yard - Newport ADJ engineers service. (John Chalcraft)

(Right) : A close up view of Class 60 No. 60099 *Ben More Assynt* boldly showing an EWS 'Beasties' sticker. The loco. is passing Worksop on September 25th heading 6T69, 13:55 Lincoln Goods Loop - Doncaster decoy ballast. (Chris Booth)

LOCOMOTIVES

60081 'Isambard Kingdom Brunel'

(Above) : This particular locomotive caught fire near Beeston on April 3rd, whilst working 6L55, Llandudno Junction - Crewe Basford Hall engineers train. After the fire brigade had finished, another Class 60 No. 60072 dragged the train back to Chester to run round and finally continue on to Crewe. (Alan Sherratt)

DRS 66/4s

(Below) : The Seaton-on-Tees flask service (6E44/6M60) is normally worked by DRS Class 20/Class 37 locomotives but on April 25th a pair of Class 66/4s Nos. 66405+66408 were diagrammed, as evidenced by the pair captured on film at Seaton Carew with 6E44, Seaton on Tees - Carlisle Yard flasks. (Ian Ball)

WHAT'S IN A NAME?

(Right) : Corporate branding is very important and Freightliner must have been disappointed to see one of their locos. No. 66612 *Forth Raider* working on the network minus its bodyside 'Freightliner' branding. This anomaly is clearly noticeable as the locomotive passes through Gospel Oak on June 9th with 6M80, Dagenham Dock - Calvert 'BinLiner'. (Iain Scotchman)

SHANKS A LOT ....

(Middle) : The distinctive Shanks-liveried Class 66/5 No. 66522 continues to find work away from its original stomping ground on the Dagenham Binliner. This was especially pleasing to the photographer when it turned up on June 28th on 6K22, Penmaenmawr - Crewe Basford Hall ballast. (Geoff Morris)

LOW EMISSION 66/9s

(Below) : Two new Freightliner locomotives entered service in 2005, built with unique low emission systems; numbered 66951 and 66952. The locomotives were originally passed for work on CTRL-2 infrastructure trains but were subsequently approved for Network Rail use.

About a month after receiving its Network Rail certification, No. 66951 approaches Welbury level crossing on June 10th with 6M25, Seaham - Earles cement empties. Welbury is located on the Eaglescliffe - Northallerton main line, which is a very busy freight route. (Ian Ball)

67029

The movements of this celebrity Class 67 locomotive are keenly followed by railway enthusiasts around the country. It is normally associated with the EWS Company Train, whose consist is a push / pull configuration with a Class 67 locomotive and MKIII DVT, finished in a distinctive livery. It was initiated in 2004 by EWS and provides a "Conference" coach with cinema and conference suites, a "Dining" coach with reception and bar area and a "Sleeper" coach containing five bedrooms, two with En-suite bathrooms.

(Above) : On this occasion, No. 67029 is seen heading the EWS train at Amington (Tamworth) on 1Z05, Lichfield - Nuneaton which had been used to take The Right Honourable Alistair Darling MP, the Transport Secretary, to Lichfield on February 22nd for a ceremony in connection with four-tracking in the Trent Valley. (Rich Norris)

(Below) : Here, No. 67029 heads past Wormit on July 16th with a Dundee - Cupar EWS Co.Train ECS move in conjunction with the Open Golf Championship at St. Andrews. The Tay Bridge is clearly visible in the background, which on the fateful night of 28th December 1879, during a violent storm, collapsed taking with it a train carrying over seventy passengers. The train fell into the murky waters of the River Tay leaving no survivors. (Jim Ramsay)

FREIGHTLINER ODDS & ENDS

(Above) : During 2005, three Class 57 locomotives were placed into store Nos. 57003, 004 and 008, of which the latter (*Freightliner Explorer*) is seen passing Lichfield on a glorious sunny day in August with 4O27, Trafford park - Southampton freightliner. (Martin Buck)

(Previous Page) : Running in multiple, Nos. 86620 *Philip G Walton* + No. 86615, heads onto the 'up' slow line at Tamworth with 4L75, Trafford Park - Felixstowe freightliner on May 12th and exactly three months after this photograph was taken, No. 86620 caught fire (see page 17) whilst working 4M74 freightliner. (Martin Buck)

(Below) : Freightliner repaints of their Class 90 fleet are not exactly taking place with any sense of urgency, which is a shame when you consider how pleasing the green and yellow livery is on the eye. Here, freshly painted in 2005, No. 90046 is near Margaretting on August 8th with 4S88, Felixstowe - Coatbridge freightliner. (Anthony Kay)

90024

(Above) : The GNER blue liveried Class 90 No. 90024 always looks good on freight duties, like in this view of it passing Crawford on August 10th with 6S50, Carlisle Yard - Millerhill departmental train. This is probably the only regular EWS 90 hauled freight, utilising daily an engine laying over at Edinburgh Waverley between Sleeper duties for a return trip to Carlisle Kingmoor. (Mark Bearton)

92013 *'Puccini'*

(Below) : It is not only non-EWS liveried diesels that are receiving EWS Logo stickers, but electrics too. Note the sticker on the bodyside of No. 92013 as it sweeps round the curve on an embankment near Lichfield with 4M41, Mossend - Daventry intermodal on December 6th. (Rich Norris)

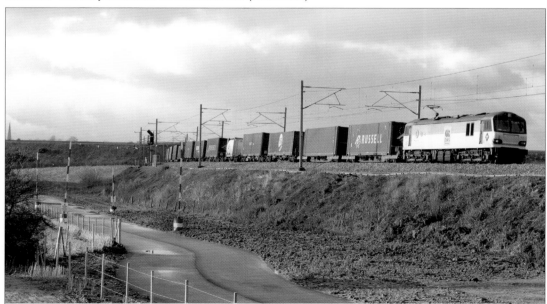

87022

(Above) : It was hoped that DRS might use Class 87 locomotives on WCML intermodal traffic but, unfortunately, this did not come to fruition. On April 11th, DRS-liveried No. 87022 leads Class 66/4 No.66410 on 4M44, Mossend - Daventry past at Hanch, near Lichfield, on an abortive Class 87 trial for DRS. (Rich Norris)

87012 *'Olympian'*

(Below) : Several members of the Class 87 fleet received new liveries and subsequently found a new lease of life when hired by GBRf to work WCML mail services; both timetabled services and Christmas mail extras. Looking back to the signalbox and level crossing, No. 87012 passes Hest Bank on August 22nd hauling 1M44, the 15:31 Shieldmuir - Warrington RMT mail, formed of two Class 325 units, Nos. 325004/014. (Alan Sherratt)

87019 'ACORP'

(Above) : The unique black-liveried Class 87 passes Badger Bridge on August 8th hauling No. 325009 on 1M44, the 15:31 Shieldmuir - Warrington RMT mail; a time when the 87 haulage regularly took place on a Monday and for the rest of the week 325 EMUs only. (Alan Sherratt)

(Below) : This close up view shows the interesting nameplate of No. 87019 *The Association of Rail Community Partnerships*', stabled one November evening. inside Warrington RMT alongside a Class 325 mail unit. (Fred Kerr)

EWS 56s & 58s ABROAD

Many rail enthusiasts visit the LGV project in France to observe ex-EWS 'grids' and 'bones' in action. Track laying on the new high speed passenger line between Paris and Strasbourg started on the "trace" of the LGV on November 2nd 2004 from the initial base at St Hilaire-au-Temple in the Champagne region of France.

The majority of the trains used to carry ballast are hauled by British Class 56 and Class 58 locomotives hired in from E.W.S. by Fertis, a subsidiary of VFLI. which is itself a subsidiary of SNCF. The track maintenance companies Seco-Rail and TSO also work out of the yard at St Hilaire-au-Temple and each has four Class 58 locomotives painted in their own liveries (Orange and Yellow, respectively).

(Above Left) : Class 56 No. 56090 brings up the rear of ballast train No. 233H near Villers Marmery.

(Below Left) : Fertis-liveried Class 58s No. 58046 and 58032 Top & Tail ballast train 132H westwards out of their St. Hillaire base.

(Above Right) : Another 'Grid', No. 56096, is seen on ballast train No. 234H near Les Petite Loges.

(Below) : Class 58s Nos. 58040+58050 pass on a sleeper train (No. 411H) near Villers Marmery, each sporting the distinctive Seco-Rail and TSO liveries.

All photographs by Iain Scotchman on July 5th.

CTRL - 2

(Above) : Construction of the second stage of the Channel Tunnel Rail Link gathers momentum and on June 11th Class 66/5 No. 66552 heads a loaded Ballast train on the CTRL-2 line at Ebbsfleet. (Iain Scotchman)

(Below) : A section of the new CTRL-2 line can be seen to the left of Class 66/6 No. 66607 with Nos. 47830+66952 DIT forming 4Z26, Dagenham - Crewe Ford car train on July 19th, departing the Ford sidings at Dagenham Dock via the new cord to Ripple Lane. (Anthony Kay)

NETWORK YELLOW

(Above) : Network Measurement Trains travel the length and breadth of the rail network using a diversity of motive power. Somewhat off the beaten track, the Network Rail yellow-liveried Class 31/1 No. 31105 brings up the rear of 4Z07, Aberdeen - Inverness NMT as No. 31106 departs Inverurie on May 9th. (Guy Houston)

(Below) : Whilst most NMTs run as one-off specials, the Network Rail HSTs ('Flying Banana') are timetabled and are listed in Freightmaster. On July 12th, the NMT HST, headed by Class 43 No. 43154, approaches Chesterfield with 1Z15, the 09:48 (TO) Leeds - Derby Etches Park with No. 443062 at the rear. (Martin Buck)

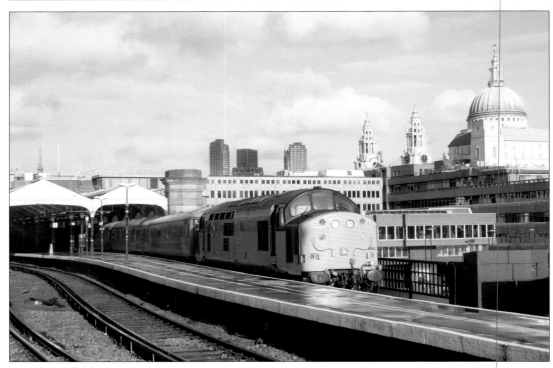

LONDON TERMINI

(Above) : With the dome of St. Paul's cathedral dominating the skyline, a rare view of diesel-hauled action at Blackfriars station on December 2nd, as EPS Class 37/6 No. 37604 and EWS Class 37/4 No. 37/427 (not visible) Top 'n' Tail 1Z14, Hither Green - Hither Green Serco Test Train. (Iain Scotchman)

(Below) : On July 14th, a Network Rail test train affords the uncommon sight of a DRS Class 37/6 locomotive, No. 37609, arriving at London Euston. No. 37616 will work the train out of the terminus. (Iain Scotchman)

WEST WALES SOJOURN

(Right) : The former Tinsley MPD flagship Class 47/0 No. 47145, heads into West Wales on August 10th with a Serco test train and is seen crossing Western Cleddau with 1Z14, East Usk - Milford Haven; No. 47355 is bringing up the rear, out of sight. (Rich Norris)

ACTON NORTH

(Middle) : Class 67s Nos. 67002 and 67022 top 'n' tail 1Z14, Derby RTC - Old Oak - Derby RTC Serco train on September 22nd at Acton North, ascending above the London Underground lines. This one-off runs at least once a year across this rarely used piece of track. (Guy Houston)

4Z10

(Below) : DRS won a contract from Serco to haul Network Rail's Ultrasonic Test Train, formed of two ex-Class 488 Gatwick Express Mk. 2f TSO vehicles (Nos. 72630 and 72631) and the ultrasonic test coach, No.999606. The train is coded 4Z10 and on November 12th it is seen crossing Fourteen Arches, Wellingborough, top 'n' tailed by Class 37/6s Nos. 37612 and No. 37607. (John Rudd)

STOCK MOVES

JGAs

(Above) : With an assortment of different rolling stock in view on June 23rd, Class 66/6 No. 66613 passes Doveholes Quarry, Peak Forest, with *FHH's* new JGA bogie hoppers forming 6E04, Tunstead - West Burton power station. (Alan Sherratt)

HIAs

(Below) : *FHH* take delivery of twenty one 90-tonne HIA aggregate hoppers built at the Wagonswidnica plant in Poland; some delivered in white livery, perhaps to be used on specific flows! On December 13th, Class 47/8 No. 47811 passes Slitting Mill, near Staveley on the 'Old Road' linking Chesterfield and Rotherham, with a complete rake of white-liveried HIAs forming 6G90, the 11:00 Doncaster Belmont - Barrow Hill. (Chris Booth)

CTAs

(Above) : One of the new CTA Brine tank wagons No. 870005 stands in Warrington Arpley Yard on February 1st en-route from the manufacturers W H Davies of Shirebrook to Oakleigh Sidings. (Alan Sherratt)

FRENCH TANKERS

(Below) : Class 66/0 No. 66110 heads 6A30, Mossend - Aberdeen 'Enterprise' past Greenhill Lower Junction on Christmas Eve with a consist made up entirely of French-registered china clay slurry tanks destined for the Croxton & Garry plant at Waterloo Quay, Aberdeen. The vehicled first appeared on 6A30 in mid-November. (Tom Noble)

STOCK MOVES

'SCRAPPERS'

(Above) : The movement of withdrawn former Eastern and Southern Region EMUs continues to retain the interest of rail enthusiasts, due in no small part that these services are hauled by non-EWS Class 66/0 locomotives. Class 66/7 No. 66713 *Forest City* is near Chalkwell with 6V91, Shoeburyness - Newport Docks 'scrapper' formed of Class 312 EMUs Nos. 312728/709 and 781. (Anthony Kay)

(Below) : The Dartmoor Railway acquired DEMU 'Thumper' sets Nos. 205028/032 from Porterbrook and are seen behind Class 66/7 No. 66708 + Class 73 No. 73204 *Janice* on January 3rd at Wyke Champflower, Somerset, looking towards Bruton and the track bed of the old S&DJR passed in the background. The train, en-route to Meldon Quarry, diverged at Castle Cary and went via Yeovil to Exeter to avoid a run round for the branch. The Class 73 was being used as a barrier vehicle. (Chris Perkins)

(Above) : The unbranded Class 47/8 locomotive No. 47830 leaves Twerton Tunnel, Bath, on April 14th with 5Z23, the 12:28 Wimbledon - Caerwent conveying Class 423 units Nos. 3405 & 3456 for scrap. (John Chalcraft)

(Below) : An interesting and unusual location for Class 66/7 No. 66711, passing Bingley on April 6th with redundant rolling stock for preservation at the Eden Valley Railway at Appleby. The location is the 'Millennium Footbridge' that crosses the Airedale line and the A650 Aire valley trunk road, which runs parallel at this point with the Leeds - Liverpool canal. The train is 6Z05, Wimbledon - Eden Valley Railway. (Mitch Thompson)

STOCK MOVES

CARTICS

(Above) : The splendid Cotswold Rail livery adorns Class 47/8 No. 47828 *Joe Strummer*, which was commandeered on August 15th to haul stored cartics from Bicester MoD to the European Metals plant at Kingsbury. The train is passing Small Heath, Birmingham, coded 6G50, Bicester - Kingsbury. (Rich Norris)

JNAs

(Below) : The unbranded 47830 is seen again, but on this occasion arriving at Long Marston on October 14th with a rake of 26 JNAs (two in view) for storage. Note, the industrial shunter on site. (Peter Tandy)

MERSEYRAIL EMUs

(Above) : Merseyrail EMUs due for refurbishment at Eastleigh Works get there using 5X61, the 12:54 (MO) Birkenhead - Eastleigh. The final Class 307 unit for refurbishment is No. 507033, which is seen in 5X91 at Dorridge on June 27th, hauled by Class 67 No. 67020. Of note is the 'X' (out-of-gauge) reporting code, but a scheduled timetabled service nonetheless. (Peter Tandy)

(Below) : On the Crewe - Chester main line, Class 67 No. 67020 passes Hargrave on June 10th towing refurbished Class 507 EMU No. 507013, forming 5X47, the 08:42 (FO) Eastleigh - Birkenhead. (Geoff Morris)

RAILHEAD TREATMENT TRAINS

RAILHEAD TREATMENT TRAINS

The Railhead Treatment Trains (RHTT), 'Water Cannons' and weedkilling trains, visit all parts of the network and are a bonus for railway photographers, as they often involve motive power working away from their normal patch. A selection of the 2005 programme is reproduced in the next few pages.

ARBROATH

(Above) : Class 66/0 No. 66111 leads 1Z95, the 03:40 Inverness - Inverness (via Aberdeen and Perth) south past the site of Elliot Junction, Arbroath, on November 19th with No. 66107 at the rear. These same two locos. worked this service continuously from early October to mdi-December. (Jim Ramsay)

CARNOUSTIE

(Below) : DRS Class 20 No. 20306 passes Golf Street, Carnoustie, on June 17th with 6Z06, Aberdeen - Carlisle Kingmoor 'weedkilling' train on its tour of Eastern Scotland; No. 20309 was on the rear. (Jim Ramsay)

COLTON JUNCTION

(Above) : One of the workings of the year took place on September 19th when GBRf Class 73s Nos. 73209 + 73206 *Lisa* hauled 6Z88, the 13:30 York - Hither Green weedkiller train seen passing Colton Junction. The train was initially delayed on departure due to an EWS shunter being unable to operate the groundframe into Klondyke Yard, York, and consequently the train only worked as far as Peterborough, before continuing on the morning of the 20th to Hither Green. (Rich Norris)

NORWICH

(Below) : The profile of a RHTT is illustrated here with DRS Class 20s Nos. 20313 and 20315 stabled at Crown Point, Norwich, on September 25th top 'n' tailing two KFA flats loaded with three NR 20-tonne water tank modules. The appearance of these trains reminds us all that the 'Sandite' season has begun! (Iain Scotchman)

RAILHEAD TREATMENT TRAINS

PRICKWILLOW

(Above) : A delightful rural composition of Class 20s Nos. 20309 and 20308 top and tailing 1Z61, the 08:43 Stowmarket - Norwich water cannon on November 4th near Prickwillow Crossing, which is on the outskirts of Ely on the Ely to Norwich main line. (Anthony Kay)

SETTLE JUNCTION

(Below) : This location just happens to be the authors favourite photographic location, Settle Junction, where Class 37s Nos. 37194 and 37229 top 'n' tail the Carnforth - Carlisle RHTT, about to come off the 'Little North Western' line from Carnforth to join the Settle & Carlisle. (Fred Kerr)

SHERBURN in ELMET

(Above) : A welcome change, a single locomotive working a RHTT, this time Class 67 No. 67005 *Queen's Messenger* approaching Sherburn in Elmet station with 6Z06, the 15:45 York Works - Doncaster new Sandite train move on September 20th. (Ian Ball)

SHREWSBURY

(Below) : DRS Class 20s Nos. 20305 and 20301 *(rear)* arrive at Shrewsbury on October 5th with 1Z96, the 13:24 Crewe Gresty Lane - Crewe Gresty Lane RHTT amidst some fine examples of GWR semaphores. (Tom Noble)

RAILHEAD TREATMENT TRAINS

STRATFORD

(Above) : Class 66/0s Nos. 66142 and 66216 (*leading*) top 'n' tail the Parkeston-based RHTT No. 2 set passing through Stratford station on October 10th. (Iain Scotchman)

WRENBURY

(Below) : This is Wrenbury on the Shrewsbury to Crewe main line, where Class 37/6 No. 37602 and Class 20 No. 20301 are seen passing on October 16th top 'n' tailing 1Z96, the 13:24 Crewe Gresty Lane - Crewe Gresty Lane RHTT via Shrewsbury, the Cambrian Line to Machynlleth, Craven Arms and Wrexham. (Alan Sherratt)